TRANSFORMATIVE THOUGHTS
for Dads

TRANSFORMATIVE THOUGHTS
for Dads

aaron pang

Author of Unstuck

Also by Aaron Pang

Transformative Thoughts for Intentional Living
Unstuck - Think Like A Kid And Free Your Mind
Reborn Digital
The Asian Dad

With arms that once held fear and pain
Now cradle joy and life again
A father, resilient, strong, and true
Through trials and triumphs, sees it through

Nappies, poonami, sleepless nights
The challenges that come with new life
But through it all, your love prevails
And steadfastly, your faith never fails

For in your embrace, a miracle thrives
A gift of life, a love that survives
And though the journey may be tough
Your love and presence will be enough

To support your partner through the rain
And give her strength to rise again
To cherish every moment, big and small
And be there to catch them when they fall

For parenting is a team sport, no less
A journey together, through every test
To support each other through the highs and lows
And be there for the moments that come and go

To share the joys and wonders of this new life
And help each other through the sleepless nights
To be a shoulder to lean on, and a guiding light
And to cherish every moment, day or night

For children are our growth cues
A reflection of the love we choose
To guide them with the right virtues
And teach them well, in all we do

To show them kindness, love, and grace
And lead them on a path to a better place
To nurture their spirits, and help them grow
Into the kind of person we want to know

For being a father is a sacred task
A chance to shape the future, and make it last
To leave a legacy, for all to see
Of the love and kindness that can set us free

So hold your child close, and never let go
For in their eyes, a love will grow
And as you guide them through life's joys and strife
You'll see the beauty of a father's life.

For being a father is a privilege rare
A chance to love beyond compare
To guide and teach, to lead the way
And watch them grow, day by day.

Respecting Vows

Don't forget your vow. It is easy
to make a lifelong commitment,
but much harder to keep one.

True Support

Help your partner succeed in their life goals. Be the light for your partner and uplift them.

Little Watchful Eyes and Ears

Never underestimate the significance
of disharmony in front of your children.
Your kids are always watching and
listening, but they might not express it.

The Great Opportunity

If you feel like you didn't have a great parent, this is your opportunity to be a great parent for someone else.

Encourage Mindfulness

Mindfulness starts young. Encourage your kids to keep a journal, put pen to paper and express their thoughts. This gives them the opportunity to reflect, learn about their emotions, and unwire any biases or assumptions they might have made about themselves or others.

Pass it Forward

Your children will want to connect with you someday when it's their turn to be parents. They will want to know about your life. They will want to learn about your struggles. They will want to know what made you who you are. Write a book. Tell them about your virtues. Tell them about your lessons learnt.

Understanding Your Child

Seek to understand before being understood. How much time do you spend on understanding your kids versus the time you expect them to understand you?

Parenting Karma

Consider that now that you are a parent, you can appreciate how hard it was raising you and keeping you alive.

Play for the Team

Parenting is a team sport, not a solo sport. You win together. You lose together.

Harmony in Parenting

Parenting is choreographing a dance together. When one person leads, the other follows. Both people need to be in sync with the same tempo.

Unresolved Issues

Conflicts are inevitable. Your enemy is the unresolved conflict, not the person who is sitting across the table.

Empathy through Knowledge

Postpartum depression is omnipresent. Read about it. Learn about it. You can't be empathetic with your other half if you don't understand it.

Growing Together

Relationships grow stronger through overcoming struggles together.

Fatherhood 2

Having a kid is your second chance to create a great father-and-child relationship.

Sowing Virtuous Seeds

Virtues are ubiquitous in kids. Compassion. Curiosity. Courage. Kindness. Your job is to sow the seeds, create an environment so that these seeds will grow into a bigger tree.

Dangerous Distractions

Beware of the distractions, noises, and
unsubstantiated marketing messages
in your environment that are trying
to clamour for your attention abou-
what's best for your children.

Be the Change You Want to See

Kids can't do it if they can't see
it. If you want to see a change
in them, start with yourself.

The Reason for Change

Kids only change for you when they are young. When they become older, they change for themselves.

Never Dismiss their Tears

when a crying grown-up comes to you, you would ask them what's wrong. when your kid comes crying at you, never tell them not to cry.

The Safe Place

Create a psychologically safe
environment so that your kids
can be vulnerable with you.

What Lies Beneath

When your child acts out, do you focus on their behaviours or are you more curious about their underlying developmental needs?

Emotions = Growth

Your kid's emotional moment
is their growth moment.

Proper Expectations

when you place grown-up
expectations on your child, you set
yourself up for disappointment
and your kid up for failure.

True Nurture

Kids are born to love and create.
Help them stay that way.

Smart Kids

Don't just focus on intellect. Your kid can never outsmart a machine. Emotional and social development are equally important.

Apologize for Losing Your Cool

Sometimes it's okay to lose your cool. You are human after all. But after you've calmed down, go back to your kid and own up to it. Tell them you're sorry your negative emotion got the better of you.

Whose Assessment Matters?

When you put your children
through a systematic funnel, it
will churn out a product that is
assessed by someone else.

Vulnerability

It is okay to admit to your kids that you made a mistake. It is okay to be vulnerable with them.

Awareness of Privilege

Be cognizant of your privileges
and teach the next generation to
have the same awareness.

Avoid Comparisons

Comparing your kids or someone else's kids in front of them is the quickest way to cause conflict in their relationship.

Sibling Preparation

Be upfront and realistic when preparing
your older child for a new sibling.
Involve the older kid with newborn
activities, nappies, feeding, bathing; you
would be pleasantly surprised how
much a three-year-old can handle.
They can be your best babysitter.

Resolving Sibling Conflict

Instead of focusing on sibling rivalry, focus on what might be fueling it. Is too much attention/praise given to one of them? Are you telling off the older child because of the younger one? How can you use more positive reinforcements instead of causing friction and resentment in their relationship?

Conflict Towards Growth

When there is a conflict between siblings, it is a growth opportunity for both of them. Don't focus on finding out who is right and who is wrong. Don't focus on penalising one party. State the problem and invite them to solve it together. If they both want to play with the same toy, mention that there is only one toy and it is not enough to share. What can we do about it? Get them to brainstorm different solutions using words and drawings. Focus on the issue, teach them to solve issues, arrive at a mutually agreeable outcome.

Different Perspectives

The world that your kid sees and the world that you see are vastly different. Your world is perceived and interpreted by your brain, which is wired in a certain way by your own experiences, lessons learnt, and biases.

Through Their Eyes

If you feel stuck, squat down to a kid's height and see what they see.

Lead by Example

Threaten a kid, and your kid will threaten others when push comes to shove. Shut down their emotions, and your kid will do the same to others. It starts with you.

Healthy Habits

Develop good habits to protect your health and your mind. If you truly love your children, try and stick around for as long as you can.

Whose Responsibility?

Saying that a kid is naughty, is going through a stormy week, or is a "terrible two" is just a way of externalising your responsibility.

Generational Progress

The next generation is always smarter
than the previous generation. They
will do things differently to you.
That's how our society improves.

Father Facilitator

You are a facilitator for your children, not a teacher. Resilience and knowing their self worth are the best gifts you can give them so that they can walk their own path.

Children Also Teach You

Your child will teach you a lot more than you think you know about yourself.

Deep vs. Shallow Relationships

In order to build a deep relationship with your child and your partner, use the following equation: presence x time spent = quality of your relationship. If you're not there mentally, you end up with a shallow relationship.

7-38-55

7% of our meaning comes from words. 38% comes from our tone, 55% comes from our body language. Pay attention to the tone of voice and body cues you use to empathise with your child. 93% of meaning comes from non-verbal cues. What do their cues say about them? Are they seeking love, attention, affirmation?

Conversation

You are always one conversation away from changing your kid's sense of self-worth. Be intentional about what you say during their emotional momen-.

Your Toolbox

A builder has many tools in their toolkit: a screwdriver, hammer, wrench, pliers, flashlight, duct tape, and so on. A parent needs more than rational reasoning to parent effectively. No child likes to be commanded what to do, constantly, 24/7. Children like to have fun and so do grown-ups.

Helicopter Parenting

Feed your child; they learn how to eat but don't know where food comes from or how to find it. Groom your chid; they learn to be neat but they don't know how to care for themselves or what to wear for which occassions. Every problem you solve for your child robs them of the opportunity to learn, be creative and independent. You raise an autopilot cnild.

Empathy

This is how to develop empathy with young children: label the emotions, not the person. Listen to their tone, watch for their non-verbal cues. 93% of their meaning is non-verbal; only 7% of it is communicated via words.

When Rationality Doesn't Work

Be silly. Be crazy. Be creative. Relive
your youth and live in your kid's world.
There is more than one way to ge- a
kid to do things. Need to put or socks?
Be the talking sock. Having difficulty
expressing their emotion? Draw it out.
Insanity is when you parent the same
way over and over again, screaming
your lungs out repeatedly, expecting
a different result each time.

Fitting in

You don't need to be like other parents to fit in. Raise resilient children to change the world, to not succumb to technologies, to not crave for external validation of their self-worth. To own up to their mistakes, learn and move on.

Dreams

"

Children don't rise to the level of their dreams. They fall to the level of resilience, compassionate sys-ems, and continual actions that give them momentum in life. Make sure they don't lose sight of their dreams.

"

The conscious possibilitarian

> Don't raise an optimist. Raise a possibilitarian, with a bedrock of hope that possibilities come from being real towards what is presented to us, and making a conscious choice to approach it freely, creatively. Teach kids about the world, the danger, the greed, the villians. Prepare them with a resilient mind to internalise growth opportunities, to make a choice on how they want to react to life. A conscious choice.

Pick Up the Phone

If you still get phone calls from your parents, thank them every time. You are lucky and should feel grateful.

Empathise with the
Older Generation

Your parents are the way they are because of their upbringing and life experiences. Given the same exposure as them, you would have behaved the same, made the same choices.

Elderly People Spend a Lot of Time Alone

Never put grandparents in the background just because you are busy with work and children.

Transforming the Past

You can't change the past but you can redefine your relationship with your upbringing, your parents.

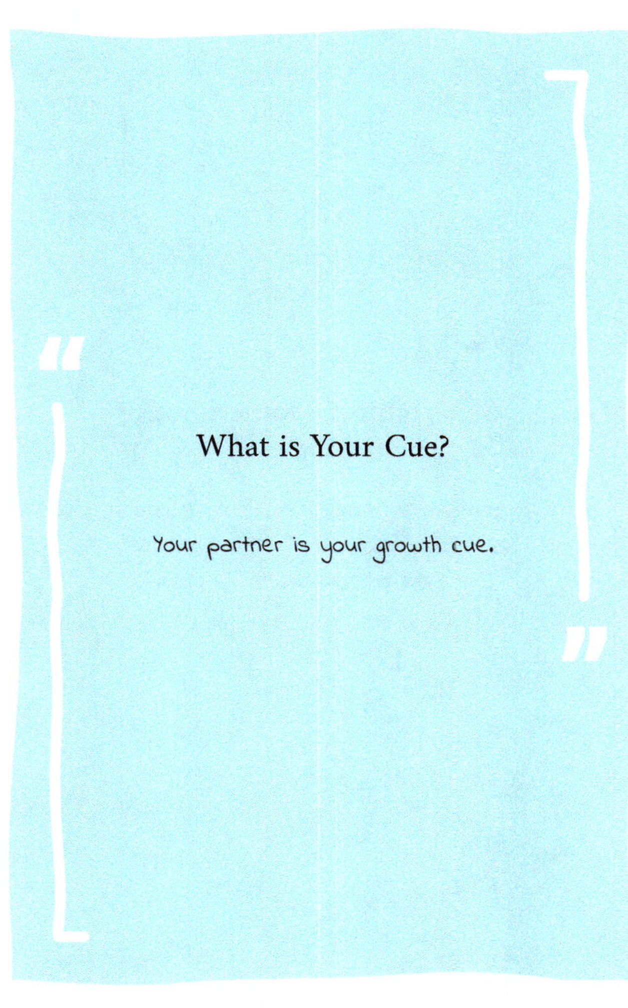

What is Your Cue?

Your partner is your growth cue.

Superhuman Motherhood

Women are superheroes. They withstand
so much physical and mental pain to
give birth to your beautiful child.

Solidifying Bonds

Set up a non-negotiable
ritual with your partner.
Spend time with your partner. Have a
date night once a week and don't let
other things get in the way. You can
only take care of your children when
you look after yourself, look after
your relationship. Remember, your
children are watching you, and they
will learn how to treat their future
partner from how you treat yours.

Peer Pressure vs. Inclusive Environment

Family portraits? Birthday parties? Tuition? Interest groups? Don't succumb to peer pressure and the cult of the "head start". Create an inclusive, safe environment where your kids can learn and explore with their curious minds.

Reassessing Your Path

Being a working parent can be men-ally draining. You are expected to be 100% at work. When you are home, you are expected to give 100% of your remaining mental reserve. If your work doesn't allow you to be 100% at home or makes you a worse parent at home, it's time to consider a differert path.

Shared Parenting Goals

When you and your partner have
a common goal in life about what
kind of children you want to raise,
the what and how become easy.

Your Power to Elevate Others

Your words and actions carry a lot of weight. It is your responsibility to use them wisely, to uplift others and communicate with positive impact.

Balanced Communication

You have two ears, two eyes and
one mouth. Use them in proportion.
Listening to speak is not the
same as listening to hear.

Personalising Love

Love your partner how they want to be loved, how they want to receive love.

Purpose of a Relationship

You are in a relationship
to give, not to take.

Challenge of Relationships

You didn't get into your relationship just for fun. You got into a relationship with your partner to get the tough going.

Beyond Merit

Love your kids the way they want
to be loved. Love shouldn't be
earnt on merit. When the going
gets tough, the love gets going.

Opinions are Allowed

others are entitled to have their
opinion about your parenting approach.
we need to be responsible for
ourselves, but we don't need -o be
responsible for their judgements.

Beware of the Cult

It is easy to fall victim to the cult of "head start" and put children in a rat race leading them to burn out.

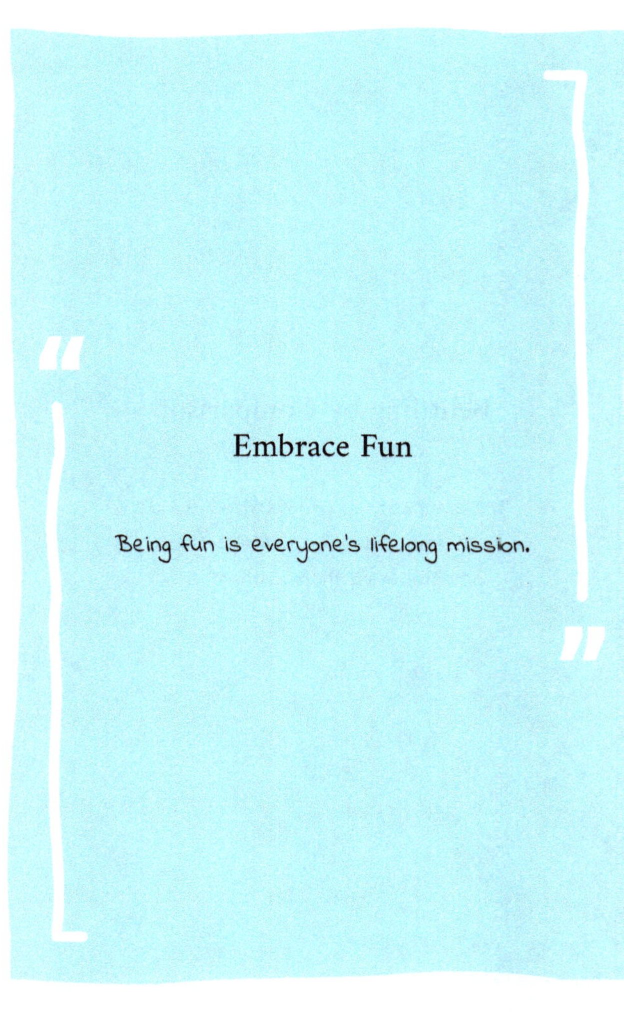

Embrace Fun

Being fun is everyone's lifelong mission.

Belittling by Comparison

The quickest way to destroy a kid's
self-esteem is by belittling them,
or comparing them with others.

Be Empathetic

Treat your kid how you would have liked to be treated when you were young.

Teach Resilience

You can't control the environment, but you can raise a resilient kid who can adapt to a changing environment.

The Screen Time Trap

If you don't want your children to suffer from attention deficit, be disciplined with screen time to avoid raising dopamine junkies.

What Makes You Happy?

Money and fame don't buy you
happiness. Teach kids early
not to join the rat race.

Address Media Influences Early

"Have frequent small chats with your children about what they have seen and heard from the media, marketing campaigns and movies. They can't fly like superheroes. They are not invincible. They don't need to beat up others they think are evil. What they get exposed to shapes their belief system. Intervene early when you see concerning behaviours, and understand the source of unkind behaviours."

Exploration, Not Naughtiness

No kid is naughty. They are merely
exploring how the world works.
You were young once, don't you
remember what you did?

Moderating Pleasure

Kids and grown-ups both enjoy
pleasures in life. We grown-ups have
learnt reasoning skills and different
tactics to get what we want.

Embrace Imperfection

No one is a perfect parent and you don't need to be one either. You are a work in progress. Develop self-awareness and identify growth opportunities to be a better parent.

Take Time

You can't care for your family
if you don't have any juice left.
Leave some time for yourself,
your partner and your friends.

What is Parenting?

The power of reframing: You don't HAVE to do parenting duties, you GET to do them.

Parenting Enhances Life

Having a child is a great way to
develop your self-awareness
and emotional intelligence.

Avoid Labels, Foster Learning

Labelling a kid by their behaviour
robs children of the opportunity
to learn and grow.

Are You Credible?

Honour your promises. Do what
you say, and walk the talk.
Hypocrisy leads to conflicts.

The Space for Epiphany

Epiphany comes from slow thinking.
Create enough mental space for
yourself to ask deliberate questions
about every day's quick thoughts.

Key Lessons

Here are some valuable lessons you can pass on to your child:
Always be curious enough to find out the unknown.
Happiness comes from within, you can't find it in the outside world.
Our quality of life comes from our own measures, not vain measures made by someone else.
Be patient and responsible for ourselves, and not for the perception and opinions others have of you.

Household Values

Five things you should demonstrate in the household:
health, positive reinforcement, gratitude, forgiveness, service.

Thinking Slow

Fast thoughts come on auto-pilot, slow
thoughts are deliberate. Your first
two thoughts are likely toxic. They are
either defensive or accusatory. Begin
and respond with your third thought.

The Gardener

Sow the seeds. water the
garden. Pick out the weeds.
Protect them from storms.

Transformative Parenting

Transformation is a result. Transformative is a process. Be a transformative parent, not a fixed parent.

Incremental Parenting

You don't rise to the level of your parenting goal. You fall to the level of your mindset, system and execution.

The Dopamine Gatekeeper

Teach your kid to think slow and live intentionally. The most important skill you can teach your kid is the ability to withstand instant gratification. Deprive them of excess materia possessions and technologies.

Choose the non-ordinary way

It's better to get stuck in parenting
extraordinarily than getting stuck
in parenting ordinarily.

One hug a day keeps
the boo boo away

when we hug, our body secre-es oxytocins associated with trust and relatonships. A 20-second hug can make stage fright dissipate. Research shows we need four hugs to survive, eight hugs to maintain the status quo and 12 hugs to grow. How often do you hug your child?

The Default

How you were treated by your parents can manifest in your parenting approach with your children. Do you know in what ways this happens?

What Can Still Be

Teach your kid to be a lifelong learner. Teach them the power of YET and let them focus on developing their craftsmanship.

Parenting Potential

Having a child is a blessing. But not having one means you could potentially foster/adopt one of your own to change someone else's future.

No Pressure

It is okay to take a raincheck
every now and then.

Parenting Food

what are you feeding your
child? Feed their ego and they
become entitled. Starve their ego
and they become humble.

Life choice

Successful people make better choices
when they are right, and when they
are wrong. Raise children so that they
can learn from their choices. Don't
rob them of the learning oppor-unity.

More Resources

Thank you for reading this book from beginning to end. I really appreciate your time and presence throughout. I would love to hear from you. Please take a picture and share your favourites with me and those who need more dopamine!

If you would like to receive updates on the latest content, you can also follow these platforms below:

Podcast: Search 'Transformative Purpose'
on your favourite podcast player.

Newsletter: Enter your email at
www.TransformativePurpose.com/Newsletter

YouTube: @TransformativePurpose

Linkedin: @AaronPang

Medium: @AaronTPang

Facebook: @TransformativePurpose

Instagram: @AaronTPang

Better together!

About Aaron Pang

It took a life-and-death encounter to throw the author off course. An event on the night of April 7th 2019 changed his life's narrative and inspired him to look inward. He felt ashamed and guilty. He saw himself as an incompetent father. Above all, he didn't know what his PURPOSE in life was. At age 35, Aaron Pang had no book, no writing experience, no podcasting experience. His negative emotions later became his greatest motivator. Aaron Pang fell in love with writing and podcasting. You're never too late to start something you love.

Aaron Pang is the author of the popular book *Unstuck - Think Like a Kid and Free Your Mind*. He is a 3-time book author, transformation coach and keynote speaker. He hosts a top 3% globally ranked podcast, Transormative Purpose. Aaron was recognised by Australia China Alumni Association as the Winner of the Australia China Alumni Award in 2022. Aaron's honest insights on success, motivation and mindset—as well as his ability to develop deep conversations—have made him a thought leader in self-improvement. His experience in business has given him a rare breadth of general management and leadership opportunities spanning across business transformation, management consulting, and entrepreneurship. Aaron lives in Hong Kong with his wife and two young boys.